Printed in Great Britain
by Amazon

36994127R00043

Series Editor Nigel Trevena

Volume Two
THE SOMERSET
& DORSET LINE

by R. C. RILEY

First published 1984
2nd impression 1985

Designed by Nigel Trevena
Printed by Century Litho, Penryn, Cornwall

© *R. C. RILEY 1984*

ISBN 0 906899 12 5

Published by
ATLANTIC TRANSPORT
PUBLISHERS
Chough House, River Street, Truro,
Cornwall, TR1 2SJ, England.

FRONT COVER: Class 2P 4-4-0 No.40563 pilots
rebuilt 'West Country' 4-6-2 No.34028 *Eddystone* at
Chilcompton Tunnel on the 6.52 am Cleethorpes-
Bournemouth West, 5th September 1959.
BACK COVER: Highbridge, 7th July 1959, with Class
3F 0-6-0 No.43436 just arrived on the 1.15 pm from
Evercreech Junction and No.43248 about to leave
with the 2.20 pm to Evercreech Junction.
THIS PAGE: Ex SDJR 2-8-0 No.53808 heads
southward, light engine, from Templecombe shed on
12th July 1960. This engine is being restored by the
Somerset & Dorset Railway Trust at Washford,
Somerset, after purchase from Barry scrapyard.

This book is dedicated to
IVO PETERS, B.E.M.

The best known feature of the S&D Line, the sharply graded section between Bath Junction and Evercreech Junction was the culmination of Somerset & Dorset Railway ambitions. The financial burden of the extension, opened in 1874, brought about the end of the S&D's independent existence when in the following year it was leased to the Midland Railway and LSWR as equal partners in a Joint Committee. The Burnham on Sea-Evercreech Junction section, the old main line of the Somerset Central Railway, reverted to branch line status and thereafter the Bath extension became the main line. The Somerset Central Railway, originally broad gauge, was linked at Cole with the standard gauge Dorset Central Railway from Wimborne, whence running powers were exercised over the LSWR to Poole and later Bournemouth. The two lines amalgamated in 1862 as the Somerset & Dorset Railway. Mixed gauge running was brought in over the Somerset Central line to simplify matters but the line became wholly standard gauge by 1870. The Bath extension changed the whole character of the line, from being a link between English and Bristol Channels to becoming a north-south rail connection, important in both World Wars.

At the 1923 Grouping the leasing arrangement ended and the Joint Committee became legally owned by the successors of the MR and LSWR — the LMS and Southern Railways. The line continued to show its independent existence, its passenger locomotives and carriages retaining the attractive Prussian Blue livery they had worn since the last decades of the 19th century. Nevertheless, it was a difficult time for railways with road traffic beginning to show an increasing dominance. On the S&D, this led to the drastic changes of 1930, the first of any consequence for over fifty years. The LMS was to be responsible for operating the line for the Joint Committee while the SR took over all maintenance and civil engineering. The locomotives were incorporated in LMS stock and the carriages went to the SR with whom they did not long survive. Highbridge Works closed, a blow to the community that grew up around it, Derby undertaking locomotive overhauls. This continued after nationalisation and for many years until the arrival of BR standard locomotives the spectacle

Class 2P 4-4-0 No.40700 pilots Class 5MT 4-6-0 No.73051 near Midford, 5th September 1959, with the 9.55 am Bournemouth-Leeds.

remained of black LMS locomotives hauling green SR coaches, one of the line's many attractive features.

After World War II a great change took place in the nation's holiday habits. Holidays with pay and petrol shortages brought travellers to the railways in large numbers in the summer months. On the S&D the peak summer service required skilful planning with most of the heavy holiday trains requiring pilot engines on the hard climb over the Mendip Hills. Southbound, the 18 mile climb to Masbury summit started at Bath Junction and, northbound, an 8 mile climb started at Evercreech Junction. There was no relaxation at the end of the southbound journey with the train engine facing Parkstone Bank unassisted. Pilot engines were attached or detached at Evercreech Junction. The Bath-Bournemouth journey was 71½ miles in length, the first half mile on MR tracks, the last 8 miles on LSWR metals. Of the 63 miles of the S&D Line, 23 consisted of three separate stretches of single line: not an easy prospect for the summer Saturday extras to run with precision, but provided southbound trains reached Bath on time everything slotted in perfectly. As well as steep gradients there were numerous curves and speed restrictions, often due to the financial stringencies of

the line's construction, and enginemen needed a high degree of skill.

The Somerset & Dorset Line was closed in 1966. With it went a line of immense character, its men serving it with great loyalty and pride despite several changes in regional boundaries after nationalisation between Southern and Western Regions, the latter becoming the most dominant and showing no interest in the line which it inherited. Nevertheless its men considered themselves as S&D men and they clung tenaciously to the line's old traditions and habits. It was this remarkable atmosphere that drew enthusiasts to the S&D in its last years.

Although I took a West Country holiday each year it was not until 1953 that I travelled on 'The Pines Express'. It was Ivo Peters' masterly photography of the line that attracted me away from the WR and SR main lines to enjoy the passing scene of the S&D and I am thankful that I did for I made many good friends, not least Ivo Peters himself in whose company some of the later pictures were taken. I am grateful to another S&D friend, Peter Smith, for his constructive comments on the captions and to Nigel Trevena for the unenviable task of making the choice of pictures from many submitted.   *RCR*

Bath Green Park

The MR line to Bristol closed in 1966 at the same time as the S&D line after which the station at Bath Green Park gradually fell into dereliction and decay even after 'Grade 2 Listed Building Status' was applied. Eventually BR sold the station to Bath City Council, having decided it was not going to be easy to sell the entire site. At the end of 1979 Bath City Council reached agreement with BR Property Board and J. Sainsbury plc permitting Sainsbury's to build a supermarket on the site of the goods yard, with allied roads and car parking, while the station was superbly restored at enormous cost. All timber has been renewed, stonework cleaned and glass panes replaced in the arched roof for the first time since the Bath blitz of 1942. The station looks magnificent, faithfully restored to original condition — if only the tracks remained and trains ran! Although Bradshaw listed the station as Bath Queen Square, it was just known as Bath until 1951 when BR added Green Park to the name. These pictures show the station in 1959.

Bath Shed

RIGHT: 0-4-4Ts formed the first addition to the Joint Committee locomotive stock after its formation in 1876. Built by the Avonside Engine Co. and Vulcan Foundry between 1877 and 1884 they were initially used as main line engines, so one envisages a lot of time spent at water columns. Attention was then turned to building 0-6-0s for the freight traffic and it was not until 1891 that 4-4-0s for main line service were introduced, remaining in various developments the mainstay of main line passenger work until bridge strengthening in 1938 permitted the use of 4-6-0s. After the LMS assumed responsibility for motive power in 1930 the surviving SDJR 0-4-4Ts were replaced on branch line work by MR Johnson 0-4-4Ts which remained until eventually LMR Ivatt 2-6-2Ts took over. No.58086, ex MR/LMS 1423, was one of the last series built in 1900 and, stored at Bath since May 1959, was the last survivor of its class when withdrawn in August 1960.

LEFT: There were two adjacent sheds at Bath, the four road SDJR shed, a wooden building, at a lower level to the stone built MR shed, which was nearer the main line. The Midland Railway was traditionally a small engine line with its Class 4F 0-6-0 design of 1911 being the largest freight engines, this design being multiplied in LMS days to a total of 772 engines. In 1914 Henry Fowler, Chief Mechanical Engineer of the MR, had designed and built six 2-8-0s specifically for use on the S&D Line. These engines could haul much heavier loads than the Class 3F 0-6-0s, hitherto the largest freight engines on the line. Nos.53803/4 were two of the original 1914 batch, seen here at Bath shed, 3rd July 1961.

Bath to Midford

LEFT. Ex SDJR 2-8-0 No 53810 climbs to Combe Down Tunnel, 26th June 1962, on a freight train from Evercreech Junction to Bath. This tunnel was a single line bore, 1,829 yards in length, the longest tunnel in the country without any ventilation. It was thus the least comfortable for enginemen and goods guards but only once was an engine crew overcome by fumes, in 1929, when an up goods train ran away and piled up at Bath, the driver of ex SDJR 2-8-0 No.89 unfortunately losing his life. The line emerged into daylight through attractive Lyncombe Vale.

BELOW: Class 4MT 2-6-0 No.76015 and Class 9F 2-10-0 No.92220 *Evening Star* approach Midford on the single line section from Bath on the 9.3 am Bristol-Bournemouth West, a train which needed no pilot engine with a Class 9F, but the Bournemouth-based 2-6-0 is attached to get it to Evercreech Junction, thus avoiding a light engine working.

Midford

LEFT: Ex SDJR 2-8-0 No.53809 (the engine involved in the Combe Down Tunnel runaway incident) crosses the eight arch Midford viaduct with a Bournemouth West-Derby empty stock train, 11th July 1960. Note the trackbed of the ex GWR Camerton-Limpley Stoke line to the right of the locomotive. No.53809 was rescued from Barry scrapyard by the late Frank Beaumont. It has been restored and has done some main line running over BR in recent years, currently being at Butterley, Derbyshire.

BELOW, LEFT: The late Signalman Percy Savage, a kind and dedicated railwayman, puts ready for action the tablet exchanging apparatus patented by Alfred Whitaker in 1905, during his 1889-1911 period as Locomotive Superintendent of the Joint Line.

Midford signal box had been rebuilt after partial demolition by errant 3F 0-6-0T No.7620 in 1936, due to the crew having failed to close the regulator and leaping from their engine to protect themselves from a collision that seemed inevitable but did not actually take place at Writhlington Colliery Sidings, near Radstock. The rebuilt Midford signal box was maintained immaculately right to the closure of the line.

BELOW: The tablet apparatus on a locomotive tender, skilfully maintained by the shed fitters to ensure reliability. This was pushed out for action and required a degree of agility by the fireman inserting and receiving the tablet. It was remarkably efficient at speed.

Class 4F 0-6-0 No.44523 assists ex SDJR 2-8-0 No.53801 on entry to the double line section at Midford with the 9.8 am Birmingham-Bournemouth West, 5th September 1959. Although at this time Class 2P 4-4-0s were the regular assistant engines, Class 4F 0-6-0s were pressed into service at times of heavy traffic. The powerful freight 2-8-0s did not appear regularly on passenger trains until the 1950s when they were allowed to take ten coaches unaided over the Mendip Hills.

The progress of this train is recorded on the following page.

LEFT: The difficulties of summer Saturday working are highlighted here as Nos.44523/53801 complete their occupation of the single line section from Bath to Midford so Class 2P 4-4-0 No.40700 and Class 5MT 4-6-0 No.73051 can proceed with the 9.55 am Bournemouth West-Leeds. LMR stock was mainly used on the north-south through trains.

ABOVE: Class 2P 4-4-0 No.40569 and rebuilt 4-6-2 No.34045 *Ottery St. Mary* with the 9.25 am Bournemouth-Manchester demonstrate the curved nature of much of the S&D line at Lower Twinhoe on the Wellow-Midford section, 12th August 1961. Part of the trackbed on this section had been laid on the course of the Radstock Tramway, which once brought coal to Midford from the

Somerset Coal Canal. The Bath extension used six miles of this tramway between Wellow and Midford, the S&D having bought it in 1871.

Wellow

ABOVE: Ex SDJR 7F 2-8-0 No.53807 sets off with a Bath freight from Wellow, having been shunted back into the siding to enable the up 'Pines Express' to pass, 6th July 1959. The 2-8-0s were built in two batches, 53800-5 (SDJR 80-5) at Derby in 1914, and a larger boilered batch 53806-10 (SDJR 86-90) from R. Stephenson & Co. in 1925. No.53809 had reverted to the smaller boiler after its 1929 accident, the remainder being similarly modified by degrees until the class was completed in 1955. When it came to No.53807's turn in 1954 the smokebox saddle was so badly corroded that it was given a new casting of 1914 design. The other rebuilds had their smokebox saddles built up to accommodate the smaller boiler.

Radstock

LEFT: Two very low bodied Sentinel shunters were ordered in 1929 to replace the ageing four coupled Radstock shunters of 1885/1895. Overall height was governed by the need to pass under the extremely low arch of Tyning Bridge, just behind Radstock signal box. Note their height compared with the Class 3F 0-6-0T. Photographed on 22nd July 1958, they were withdrawn in 1959 and 1961, by which time the arch had been demolished.

Midsomer Norton

Class 3F 0-6-0T No.47316 (ex SDJR No.25), last of the six built for the SDJR by Bagnalls in 1929 to remain on the line, has added its load of coal wagons from Norton Hill Colliery to the train of Class 7F 2-8-0 No.53810, which it piloted down to Radstock, its home shed. Note the flower basket on Midsomer Norton signal box, a feature for which this station was particularly noted, although flowers were tended on most stations on the line. 3rd July 1961.

Norton Hill Colliery

BELOW: One source of the S&D line coal traffic. A typical product of Pecketts of Bristol, 1906 built *Lord Salisbury* shunts the sidings at Norton Hill Colliery, near Midsomer Norton station on 3rd July 1961. The colliery was closed less than a month before the S&D line. A few years earlier *Lord Salisbury's* green Peckett livery was immaculately maintained and the dome and spring balance safety valve highly polished. The S&D line ran beside the colliery at a lower level.

RIGHT: Just about the least scenic part of the S&D line, Class 4MT 4-6-0 No.75072, in double chimney form, passes a colliery slag tip near Midsomer Norton on the 3.20 pm Bath-Templecombe, 1st July 1961. According to my notes the previous photograph showed a Somerset Fire Brigade fire tender leaving the scene. As the vegetation shows, it had been a long dry period and the passing of Nos.40634/ 34047 *Callington* vigorously tackling the climb on the late running down 'Pines

Express' had started some lineside fires, the 'West Country' being the worst offender. One fire was dangerously near a timber store in the colliery sidings but fortunately was quickly extinguished.

Near Chilcompton

BELOW: Class 4MT 4-6-0 No.75027 and 4-6-2 No.34041 *Wilton* head the 10.38 am Manchester-Bournemouth West, near Chilcompton, 9th July 1960. The first Class 4MT 4-6-0s to reach the line were Nos.75071-3 in 1956 but after the WR took over they transferred in several more, which largely eliminated the less suitable Class 4F 0-6-0s from passenger working. No.75027 is now preserved on the Bluebell Railway.

ABOVE: On a Saturday when locomotive availability was at a low ebb Class 2P 4-4-0 No.40569 pilots Class 4F 0-6-0 No.44422 on the 7.0 am Cleethorpes-Exmouth approaching Chilcompton tunnel. The Exmouth train had started in 1929 but on its revival after the war it ran for a few years into Bournemouth. Templecombe shed often provided a Bath based Class 7F 2-8-0 for the up working. This was at a time when there was an abundance of carriage stock available for the Saturday workings and several of the through trains over the S&D would do a single journey and then wait in carriage sidings at either destination point until the following Saturday.

RIGHT: Class 4F 0-6-0 No.44102 heads the 4.15 pm Templecombe-Bath near Chilcompton tunnel, 9th July 1960. The stock consists of three SR Maunsell corridors, usual at this date. The Class 4F 0-6-0s were not really suitable passenger engines and apart from being rough riding they were prone to axlebox overheating.

Masbury Summit

Class 7F 2-8-0 No.53809 approaches
Masbury summit with the 8.55 am Bath-
Evercreech Junction freight, banked by
Class 3F 0-6-0T No.47496, 6th October
1962. Freight trains were suspended on
Saturdays in the summer service. The
Class 7F 2-8-0s were fitted with the
same Fowler axlebox design as the Class
4Fs but they did not suffer hot boxes to
the same extent. They were very
powerful engines and latterly fitted with
Ferodo brake linings for longer wear.
Note that the engine is blowing off at the
summit of the climb.

ABOVE: Masbury summit, 811 feet above sea level, is clear in this picture of Class 4MT 4-6-0 No.75073 heading the 2.45 pm Bournemouth West-Bristol, 18th July 1959. Much of the gradient on either side of the summit was at 1 in 50.

LEFT: Class 4F 0-6-0 No.44422 pilots Class 5MT 4-6-0 No.73050, having just surmounted Masbury summit with the 10.5 am Bournemouth West-Derby, 9th July 1960. The weather was quickly changeable on the Mendip Hills and summer Saturday pictures were often made more difficult with clouds rapidly gathering. Class 5MT 4-6-0s of BR design replaced the SR Bulleid light Pacifics in 1954 and were very popular. Both these engines have been preserved: No.44422 was rescued from Barry scrapyard and is now at Cheddleton, Staffordshire, while No.73050 was bought out of service and now runs on the Nene Valley Railway near Peterborough.

Guard's eye view of the Masbury banker, in this case No.47557, on 26th September 1959. Southbound freight trains were banked out of Bath, the banker collecting the 'Bath Banking Engine' staff at Bath Junction and passing through Devonshire Tunnel, dropping back as the gradient changed before Combe Down Tunnel. Then at Radstock the Masbury banker was coupled on for the climb to the summit. At Binegar the banker picked up a wrong line staff by means of its tablet catcher for its return working light. Just before Masbury summit, with the aid of the hook seen on No.47557's smokebox, the Goods Guard would uncouple the banker and it would return light to Radstock, regaining the up line at Binegar, where the staff was surrendered. On northbound freights there were more empty wagons on the train and these were not sufficiently heavy to require banking, especially after 1959 when the WR diverted much of the freight traffic away from the S&D. However, two night freights, the 10.0 pm and 12.30 am from Evercreech Junction, usually required banking and an engine rostered for the task. When extra banking was necessary, as at Bath, the yard shunting engine would be used. The trains then made a brief stop at Binegar to release the banker. Night freights on the S&D were discontinued in September 1964.

Shepton Mallet

Ex SDJR 7F 2-8-0 No.53805 pauses to take water at Shepton Mallet on the 12.35 pm freight from Bath, having surmounted Masbury, 26th September 1959. Two arches of the down line of Charlton Viaduct, approaching the station, collapsed in 1946 causing problems until they were rebuilt. This was a reminder that the line was once wholly single, the up side viaduct, being separate, remaining intact. The tunnels at Chilcompton and Winsor Hill similarly comprise bores built at different times. Apart from a brief climb out of Shepton Mallet to pass over the ex GWR Witham-Wells-Yatton branch, the gradient fell to Evercreech Junction.

Evercreech New

For the summer seasons of 1960-2 the WR transferred four 9F 2-10-0s to the line and these could manage 410 tons between Bath and Evercreech Junction unassisted. This greatly alleviated the Saturday motive power situation, but they were not retained outside the summer service as they were not fitted for steam heating trains. After the 1962 summer service the WR diverted through trains away as part of the run down of the S&D system. Here the Evercreech New porter watches No.92001 as it starts the climb to Masbury with the 10.32 am Bournemouth West-Manchester, 28th July 1962. In the late summer of 1963 two Class 9Fs came back for a short spell to alleviate an engine shortage. The 9Fs were confined to Bath-Bournemouth through trains as they were too large for the turntable at Evercreech Junction.

Evercreech Junction

ABOVE: Evercreech Junction station, which often deservedly won awards for the Best Kept Station competition. The oldest buildings are those furthest from the camera and the large water tank beyond the tall starting signal carried a cast iron plate reading 'S.&D.R. Wimbledon Ironworks 1892', a reminder of the LSWR's partnership. All trains stopped at Evercreech Junction latterly, in the case of expresses often to attach or detach an assisting engine. On a summer Saturday the centre road was occupied by pilot engines, usually Class 2P 4-4-0s but latterly BR Class 4MT 4-6-0s, ready for the northbound climb.

RIGHT: Ivatt 2-6-2T No.41296 waits in the middle road at Evercreech Junction with two empty coaches to form a Highbridge train, 6th July 1959. It will set back into the platform to provide a connection after departure of a Bath train. In latter years, these 2-6-2Ts were the most popular branch engines, having replaced the Johnson 0-4-4Ts. Two were allocated to Templecombe in 1953, the allocation increasing over the years.

ABOVE: Clearly showing that it is 'The Pines Express', the down train pauses at Evercreech Junction. Class 5MT 4-6-0 No.73087 is taking water while the assistant engine, Class 2P 4-4-0 No.40652, is being uncoupled to return to Templecombe shed. The old station building is just evident in this picture, 6th July 1959. A service between Manchester/Liverpool to and from Bournemouth was introduced in October 1910 over the S&D route but it was not named 'The Pines Express' until 1927. Its loading then was six coaches to keep it within the limitations for a 2P 4-4-0 over the S&D line. It ran daily except Sundays and even in duplicate on ordinary weekdays. Withdrawn on the outbreak of war it was reinstated in

1949. After bridge strengthening on the Mangotsfield-Bath line in 1938, Stanier Class 5MT 4-6-0s were permitted to work on the S&D on which bridge strengthening had been carried out five years earlier. These could haul 270 tons unassisted on the graded part of the line as could the BR 5MT 4-6-0s which eventually replaced both them and the Bulleid Pacifics.

LEFT: Class 5MT 4-6-0 No.73028 ready to leave Evercreech Junction with a brake van only for Bath. This shows the layout at the north end of the station, the Highbridge branch, once the Somerset Central Line, coming in dead straight, while the Bath extension curves sharply to the right. The backing signal was a distinctive feature of the S&D and in this case was to enable freight trains from Bath to back into the sidings adjacent to the Highbridge line. 6th July 1959.

ABOVE: Evercreech Junction on the same day. 'West Country' 4-6-2s: No.34043 *Combe Martin* on the down 'Pines Express' relief passes No.34044 *Woolacombe* on an up empty stock train. Bulleid light Pacifics were first allocated to the line in 1951. Their suitability was soon put into doubt when their slipping propensities became apparent, but although they ceased to be allocated to Bath members of the class continued to work on the line from the Bournemouth end. BR rebuilds of the class first appeared on the line in 1959. Their maximum load between Bath and Evercreech Junction was 270 tons, the same allowance as that for the Class 5MT 4-6-0s.

RIGHT: It was not until November 1963 that BR Class 4MT 2-6-4Ts were used on the line from Bournemouth but by this time the through trains had been diverted away and the surviving passenger service consisted solely of stopping trains. These were ideal engines in the reduced circumstances of the line. No.80043 was recorded near Wyke Champflower on 3rd July 1965.

BELOW: Class 3F 0-6-0 No.43218 (ex SDJR No.73) near Cole on 18th July 1959 with the 4.19 pm milk train from Highbridge. The milk came from a factory at Bason Bridge 1½ miles up the branch from Highbridge and was destined for SR London depots via Templecombe. Later in WR days the milk went out via that region's station at Highbridge, to which there was always a connection and at which location the S&D line to Burnham-on-Sea crossed the WR Bristol-Taunton main line on the level.

Cole

Class 4F 0-6-0 No.44422 enters Cole on the 4.37 pm Bath-Templecombe, 18th July 1959. Cole was of importance in having been the meeting place of Somerset Central and Dorset Central lines, the building representing the latter company's architectural style. Just north of the station the line crossed the WR main line between Westbury and Taunton, west of Bruton, and in BR days the stationmaster at Cole also had charge of the WR station at Bruton. Cole's contribution to the S&D's floral display included a goldfish pond! The five arch bridge over the WR line is seen in the previous picture. No.44422 has been rescued from Barry scrapyard and is undergoing restoration at Cheddleton, Staffs.

As the WR increased its influence on the line so ex GWR Collett 0-6-0s were transferred to replace the 3F 0-6-0s, the last of which was withdrawn in 1962. Collett No.2277 leaves Cole on the 2.20 pm Highbridge-Evercreech Junction, 1st September 1962. As WR branches became dieselised or closed so these 0-6-0s would be transferred to the line, often for only a few months before withdrawal. Much of their work was typical 3F work on the Highbridge line, where the drivers preferred the Ivatt 2-6-2Ts which remained at closure. WR 0-6-0s were on the line from 1960 to 1965. Note, too, that the branch train is formed of ex GWR coaches. The headlamp code for passenger trains, whether express or local, was the same, another feature of S&D individuality.

Shepton Montague

RIGHT: Another displaced engine, No. 34103 *Calstock,* which spent most of its working life on the ex-LCDR lines to East Kent, electrified in 1959. It is seen at Shepton Montague between Cole and Wincanton on 1st September 1962 working the 12.20 pm Bournemouth West-Nottingham. Only a week later the last north-south expresses ran over the S&D and from then on the line was reduced to local services only, with the occasional excursion or enthusiast special to relieve the monotony.

ABOVE: 9F 2-10-0 No.92233 heads the 7.45 am Bradford-Bournemouth West near Shepton Montague, 1st September 1962. This engine and the other 9F 2-10-0s were transferred away that month.

LEFT: Engineer's occupation at Wincanton, 16th July 1961, work which had to be restricted to Sundays. There is just a glimpse through the goods shed of the engineer's train, mainly ballast wagons with a Scottish Region coach heading the formation as the mess coach. The engine in charge was Class 7F No.53810.

Templecombe

From 1870, with the construction of the Salisbury & Yeovil Railway operated by the LSWR, a new and rather steep spur line was built from Templecombe No.2 signal box to the West of England line station, where S&D trains ran into a platform on the north side of the up main platform. A new Templecombe Lower platform was provided near the point where the S&D line passed under what became the main LSWR line to the West

Country, but this was little used. It was quite a performance to get up to the SR line and involved use of a pilot engine. Thus, while trains from Bath could run straight into Templecombe they needed the services of the pilot engine to return them to Templecombe No.2 signal box and so on to the S&D line heading for Bournemouth. Similarly, trains from Bournemouth would stop for the pilot to be attached to haul them into the SR station. Templecombe No.1 signal box was near the old Dorset Central station but was not closed until 1887, although

little used after the spur line was built. Templecombe No.3, at Horsington Crossing, controlled entry into the lower yard and engine shed. It closed in 1933, its functions being taken over by No.2 box, which although the only surviving box was No.2 box to S&D men to the end of the line.

Here, 3F 0-6-0 No.43248 (ex-SDJR No.75) hauls the 3.40 pm Bournemouth-Bristol up to the SR station on 7th July 1959, 4MT 4-6-0 No.75072 being the train engine. Note the tablet catcher for northbound trains.

BELOW: Class 5MT 4-6-0 No.73052 heads the 4.16 pm stopping train Evercreech Junction-Bournemouth West past Templecombe shed, 7th July 1959. The tall building used as motive power offices was formerly the Dorset Central station. The engine shed was rebuilt in 1950. Note the tablet catcher on the tender of Class 2P 4-4-0 No.40634 (ex SDJR No.45), withdrawn two years later as were all but one of the other 4-4-0s remaining on the S&D.

RIGHT: Class 9F 2-10-0 No.92220 *Evening Star,* now well known in the National Collection, preserved as the last steam locomotive built at Swindon, stands by Templecombe No.2 box awaiting its signal to proceed to Bournemouth West on the 9.3 am Bristol, 1st September 1962. It had been hauled from the station by WR 0-6-0PT No.3758. The following Saturday *Evening Star* worked the last up and down 'Pines Express' trains before their diversion away from the S&D line. Unexpectedly, Nos.92220 and 92224 returned to the S&D in the late summer of 1963 because of an engine shortage. By this time train loads were greatly less than the power of these engines warranted.

LEFT: Newly overhauled Class 4F 0-6-0 No.44559, one of five members of its class built for the SDJR by Armstrong Whitworth in 1922 as Nos.57-61, becoming LMS Nos.44557-61. It is heading the 4.16 pm Evercreech Junction-Bournemouth West on 12th July 1960, this train providing a connection to intermediate stations for the down 'Pines Express'. The pilot engine that has brought the train from Templecombe SR can be seen in the distance at the signals close to Templecombe No.2 box.

BELOW: Class 4MT 4-6-0 No.75072 on the 3.40 pm Bournemouth West-Bristol at Templecombe, 7th July 1959. The spur line it will use to reach Templecombe SR can be seen at the right. The old Dorset Central line had been nearer to the present goods yard. Note the predominance of SR (and even ex-LSWR) carriage stock.

Sturminster Newton

ABOVE: Class 9F 2-10-0 No.92220 *Evening Star* crosses the River Stour north of Sturminster Newton on the 3.40 pm Bournemouth West-Bristol, 1st September 1962. The relatively level line of the former Dorset Central Railway in attractive pastoral country was in complete contrast to the north end of the line and one of the scenic features of the S&D.

RIGHT: Ivo Peters and the late Norman Lockett wave to the crew of 'West Country' 4-6-2 No.34043 *Combe Martin* on the down 'Pines Express', 1st September 1962. The up 'Pines' left Bournemouth at 9.45 am and the down train left Manchester at 10.25 am. By this time the Bournemouth Pacifics were beginning to look rather neglected and, indeed, withdrawals started the following year, only two surviving to see the end of steam on the SR in July 1967. Two, Nos.34006 *Bude* and 34057 *Biggin Hill* were beautifully groomed to work the LCGB Farewell Tour over the S&D line on 5th March 1966, the last trains running on the following day.

Near the end of the line

TOP: Class 4F 0-6-0 No.44557 at Bailey Gate on the 6.35 am Evercreech Junction-Poole pick up goods, which until 1959 made occasional forays up the remains of the old Dorset Central branch to collect clay wagons from Carters Siding. Class 4MT 4-6-0 No.75027, now preserved on the Bluebell Railway, is

approaching on the 11.40 am Bournemouth West-Bristol, 4th July 1961.
ABOVE LEFT: Class 9F 2-10-0 No.92000, pioneer of the class, near Corfe Mullen on the 9.3 am Bristol-Bournemouth West, 4th July 1961. The train is on the Bailey Gate-Broadstone direct line opened in 1885. This three mile line obviated the nuisance of reversal at Wimborne and reduced the line's overall mileage by three miles by so doing. Wimborne lost its passenger traffic

in 1920 and the short length from Corfe Mullen to the clay siding was all that remained from 1933 to 1959. This track at right had not by then been lifted.
ABOVE RIGHT: Broadstone, the southernmost point of the S&D line, beyond which trains travelled over ex-LSWR lines to Bournemouth West, including the short but severe climb of Parkstone bank. The single S&D line can be seen curving away to the left of the signal box, 4th July 1961.

S & D Branches

ABOVE: Highbridge East on 7th July 1959. Class 3F 0-6-0 No.43248 (ex SDJR No.75) heads the 2.20 pm Evercreech Junction. The Johnson 0-6-0s took number 'blanks' on the MR/LMS locomotive list in 1930.

Burnham on Sea lost its passenger service in 1951 and freight traffic in 1963, so Highbridge was the latter day terminus of the branch. Once the Somerset Central main line, it was 24 miles in length, mostly flat but climbing Pylle bank beyond West Pennard before the Junction.

Most of the S&D locomotive works buildings at Highbridge, closed in 1930, remained intact, although derelict, when the line closed in 1966.

BELOW: Glastonbury station, apart from the loss of its track, looking remarkably intact in 1977, eleven years after closure. This had been the headquarters of the Somerset Central Railway, and for a time the S&D, until control was transferred to Bath in 1877. The buildings included engineers' workshops, and offices serving the once busy goods yard. The Wells branch, built three years before the line to Evercreech Junction, came into the outer face of the down platform until closure in 1951. The only other S&D branch, opened in 1870, ran from Edington Junction, seven miles west of Glastonbury, to Bridgwater, but this lost its passenger traffic in 1952.